DISCOVERING SCIENCE

ENERGY

Rebecca Hunter

www.raintreepublishers.co.uk
Visit our website to find out more information about **Raintree** books.

To order:
☎ Phone 44 (0) 1865 888112
▤ Send a fax to 44 (0) 1865 314091
▢ Visit the Raintree Bookshop at www.raintreepublishers.co.uk to browse our catalogue and order online.

First published in Great Britain by Raintree,
Halley Court, Jordan Hill, Oxford
OX2 8EJ, part of Harcourt Education.

Raintree is a registered trademark of Harcourt Education Ltd.

© Harcourt Education Ltd 2003
First published in paperback in 2004
The moral right of the proprietor has been asserted.

Produced for Raintree by Discovery Books Ltd
Design: Ian Winton
Editorial: Rebecca Hunter
Consultant: Jeremy Bloomfield
Commissioned photography: Chris Fairclough
Illustrations: Keith Williams, Jenny Mumford and Stefan Chabluk
Production: Jonathan Smith

Originated by Dot Gradations Ltd
Printed and bound in China by South China Printing Company

ISBN 1 844 21567 9 (hardback)
07 06 05 04 03
10 9 8 7 6 5 4 3 2 1

ISBN 1 844 21574 1 (paperback)
08 07 06 05 04
10 9 8 7 6 5 4 3 2 1

British Library Cataloguing in Publication Data
Hunter, Rebecca
Energy. – (Discovering Science)
530
A full catalogue record for this book is available from the British Library.

Acknowledgements
The publishers would like to thank the following for permission to reproduce photographs:
Bruce Coleman: page **17** top (P. Kaya), Discovery Picture Library: page **11** bottom, **27**; Chris Fairclough: page **8** bottom, **15** (all), **26** top; Oxford Scientific Films: page **19** bottom; Science Photo Library: page **8** (Kent Wood), **11** top (Michael Marten), **18** (Chris Butler), **19** top (Astrid & Hanns-Frieder Michler), **21** (Martin Bond), **23** top (Ton Kinsbergen), bottom (Alex Bartel), **24** (David Parker); gettyimages: page **4** top (James Andrew Bareham), bottom (Arnulf & Hild), **5** (Patrick Donehue), **10** (Peter Cade), **14** left (John Warden), right (Lori Adamski Peek), **16** (Chad Slattery), **17** bottom (Manoj Shah), **20** (Ken Graham), **22** (Nicholas DeVore), **26** bottom (Dave Jacobs), **28** (Hideo Kurihara), **29** (Ragnar Sigurdsson).

Cover photograph of particles in motion reproduced with permission of Science Photo Library.

The publishers would like to thank the following schools for their help in providing equipment, models and locations for photography sessions: Bedstone College, Bucknell, Moor Park, Ludlow and Packwood Haugh, Shrewsbury.

Every effort has been made to contact copyright holders of any material reproduced in this book.
Any omissions will be rectified in subsequent printings if notice is given to the publishers.

Any words appearing in the text in bold, **like this**, are explained in the Glossary.

CONTENTS

WHAT IS ENERGY?

What makes things happen? What makes a volcano erupt? What makes a sailing boat move? What makes birds fly and fish swim? What allows you to run around, play and laugh?

Energy makes these things happen. Without energy there would be nothing. The universe would be cold and still. Nothing would move. Nothing would grow. Nothing would live. But what is energy? Where does it come from?

Scientists describe energy as the ability to cause change or movement. Energy comes from lots of different places. A racehorse uses energy from food to run. Energy in moving air makes a kite fly. A rocket has energy stored in its fuel that enables it to fly into space.

A racehorse needs a lot of energy to win the race.

FORMS OF ENERGY

You can see energy at work in many forms.

SOUND ENERGY

The human voice gives off sound energy.

ELECTRICAL ENERGY

Some toys are powered by electrical energy. Electrical energy provides the power to make many machines work.

LIGHT AND HEAT ENERGY

The Sun gives off enormous amounts of both light and heat energy.

MOVEMENT ENERGY

These children on bicycles have movement energy.

CHEMICAL ENERGY

Fuels store chemical energy. This energy can be used to power a car.

CHANGING ENERGY

The amount of energy in the universe is always the same. Energy cannot be created, or destroyed– but energy can change from one form into another. For example, when a bolt of lightning strikes, electrical energy is changed into light, sound and heat energy.

◀ Chemical energy in the clock's battery changes into movement. It is this movement energy that turns the clock's hands.

PROJECT

This experiment shows how forms of energy change.

You will need:
a large candle
a large needle
matches
a small circle of aluminium foil.

1. Cut eight slits in the foil circle.

Bend the strips of foil up slightly to make a pinwheel.

2. Push the needle into the top of the candle.

3. Make a small dent in the centre of the pinwheel and balance it on top of the needle.

4. Ask an adult to light the candle with a match.

! ASK AN ADULT TO HELP YOU WITH THIS EXPERIMENT.

5. The pinwheel should turn. Can you identify the changing forms of energy?

CHEMICAL (in the match) → is changed into → **HEAT** (from the candle heating the air) → which is changed into → **MOVEMENT** (of the pinwheel)

MOVEMENT ENERGY

There are two types of movement energy: **kinetic energy** and **potential energy**.

KINETIC ENERGY

Kinetic energy is energy in use. Anything that is moving or changing has kinetic energy.

Blowing wind has kinetic energy.

Flowing water has kinetic energy. If a twig falls into a river, it too will have kinetic energy, transferred to it by the moving water.

These children playing in the pool have kinetic energy.

POTENTIAL ENERGY

Potential energy is stored energy. Something has potential energy when it is not moving, but it is in a position to move. If you hold a marble in the air, it has potential energy. If you drop the marble, it has **kinetic energy** as it falls.

1. The girl on this diving board has potential energy.

2. When she dives off the board, her potential energy changes into kinetic energy.

3. When the diver hits the water, her kinetic energy is turned into sound, heat and movement of the water.

Somebody on a higher diving board would have more potential energy than the girl. This is because they have climbed higher and have further to fall.

PROJECT

Can you identify whether the things in these pictures have potential or kinetic energy?

You will find the answers at the bottom of the page.

1. Skier at the top of a slope

2. Skier racing down a slope

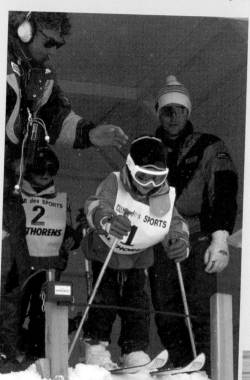

3. Racing car at full speed

Answers: **1.** Potential energy **2.** Kinetic energy **3.** Kinetic energy

13

STORED ENERGY

Stored chemical energy is a type of **potential energy**. Plants store energy in their leaves and roots. Then, they use it for growth and to produce flowers and seeds. The stored energy in plants is passed on to animals when they eat them.

Animals store chemical energy in their muscles and body fat. They use this mainly for growth and movement.

Every time you move you are changing your stored chemical energy into movement energy and heat energy. The more you move, the hotter you get!

Playing sports uses up your stored energy and changes it into movement and heat.

FUEL AND BATTERIES

The energy stored in fuel runs our cars and heats our homes. It also provides the electricity that powers the many machines we use each day.

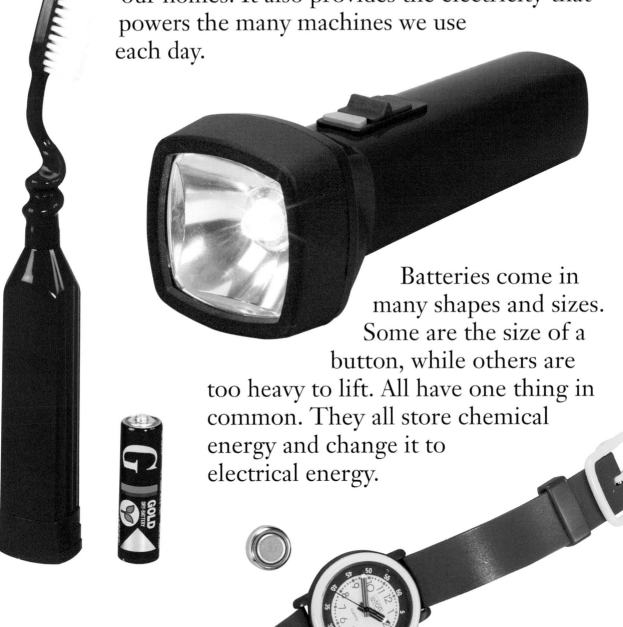

Batteries come in many shapes and sizes. Some are the size of a button, while others are too heavy to lift. All have one thing in common. They all store chemical energy and change it to electrical energy.

ENERGY FROM FOOD

Humans get their energy from food. The amount of energy a person needs depends on their age and how active they are. A baby needs less energy than a child. A very active adult, such as an athlete or builder, needs more energy than an elderly, retired person.

A BALANCED DIET

To stay healthy, a person needs to eat certain foods. These foods provide the right amount of energy and enough fibre, vitamins and minerals.

Eating a healthy breakfast is a good start to the day.

Different foods contain different amounts of energy. Foods that are made of fats have the most energy, but they are not the best for you. Foods with lots of sugar, starch or protein have less energy.

Plants like grasses have lots of starch and fibre. Animals that eat only plants have to eat large amounts of food to get all the energy they need.

▲ A horse will spend most of its day grazing.

Meat has lots of protein and fat. As a food, it provides more energy than plants. That is why **carnivores**, like lions, do not need to eat as often as other animals.

◄These lions will not need more food for several days after they have feasted on a kill.

SOURCES OF ENERGY

ENERGY FROM THE SUN

Most energy on Earth comes from the Sun. The Sun gives off huge amounts of energy as heat and light. Some of this energy reaches Earth. More energy reaches Earth from the Sun in one hour than all of us use in a year!

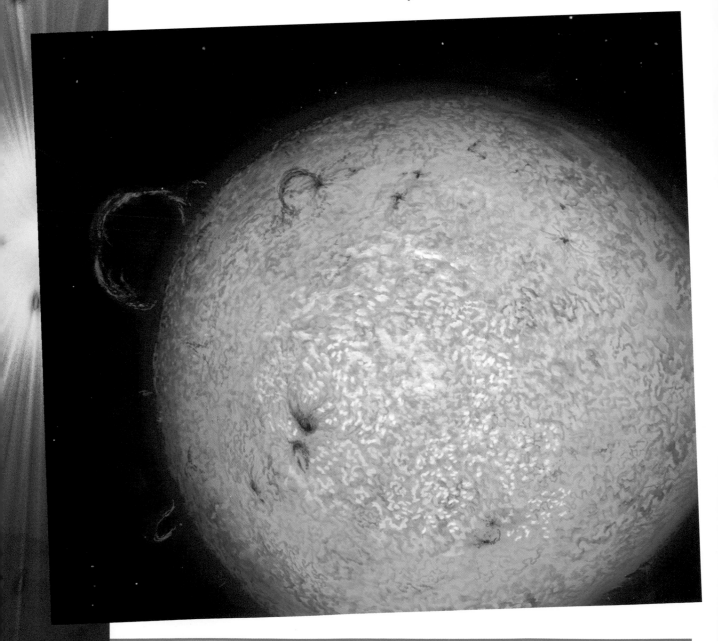

THE ENERGY CHAIN

The Sun's light and heat that reach Earth are the first step in the energy chain that supports all the life on our planet. Plants are able to use the energy in sunlight to make their own food from **chlorophyll**. This process is called **photosynthesis**.

Plants need chlorophyll in their leaves to change sunlight into energy.

The light energy from the Sun is changed to chemical energy in food. Plants store some of this chemical energy. When plants are eaten by animals, energy in the plants is passed on to the plant eaters. Some animals eat plant-eating animals, and the energy is passed on again.

Fossil fuels

Coal, gas and oil are known as **fossil fuels**. They were formed from the remains of plants and animals that died millions of years ago. Sunlight used by these plants to make food, which then fed the animals, was stored in the plants and animals as chemical energy.

Fossil fuels are used to produce electrical energy, or electricity, in power stations. The power stations burn coal, gas or oil to make heat. The heat boils water to make steam that turns **turbines**. Turbines power machines that change movement energy into electrical energy.

So even electrical energy can be traced back to the Sun. You use the energy in electricity in your home – but this energy really arrived on Earth in sunlight millions of years ago.

Drilling for oil under the sea.

Energy flow

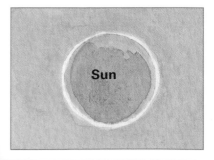

Sun

Ancient forests grew using the Sun's energy.

The forests turned to fossils underground.

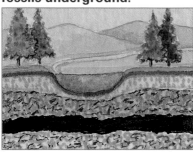

FOSSIL FUELS AND POLLUTION

The burning of fossil fuels **pollutes** our environment – our air, our water and the natural world around us. Our current supplies of fossil fuels will only last for another 250 years. So scientists are looking for new sources of energy to fuel industries and homes. There are several other forms of natural energy that are safe and clean.

This power station has been fitted with equipment to reduce pollution.

The fossil remains of plant matter are mined as coal.

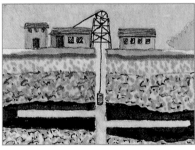

Electricity is generated from burning coal.

Electricity can be used in many ways.

WIND POWER

The power of the wind has been used as a source of energy for hundreds of years. Sailing ships once took people and goods all around the world.

This sailing ship shows how people and goods once travelled.

Windmills were once used to drive machines.

▶ *The sails of these mills once turned great millstones that ground wheat grains into flour.*

Modern wind farms have rows and rows of wind **turbines**. These turbines use the energy of the wind to drive electricity **generators**. Wind turbines do not create pollution. Although some people who live near them do not like the noise they make.

These turbines are part of a modern wind farm in California, USA.

WATER POWER

Moving water is also a major source of energy. At a **hydroelectric power** (HEP) plant, a river is dammed to create a lake. The lake is a **potential energy** source. When the water is allowed to flow through the dam, a **generator** changes the **kinetic energy** of the flowing water into electrical energy. Many large HEP dams have been built all over the world to use this natural energy. About one fifth of the world's electricity comes from hydroelectric power.

The Hoover Dam HEP plant is built across the Colorado River in the USA.

Every day the level of the oceans rises and falls. This movement is called the tide. It is possible to use the tides to provide HEP. This means building a power plant must be built across the lower part of a river where it meets the tides. As the tides flow in and out, reversible **turbines** that work in both directions drive generators to make electricity.

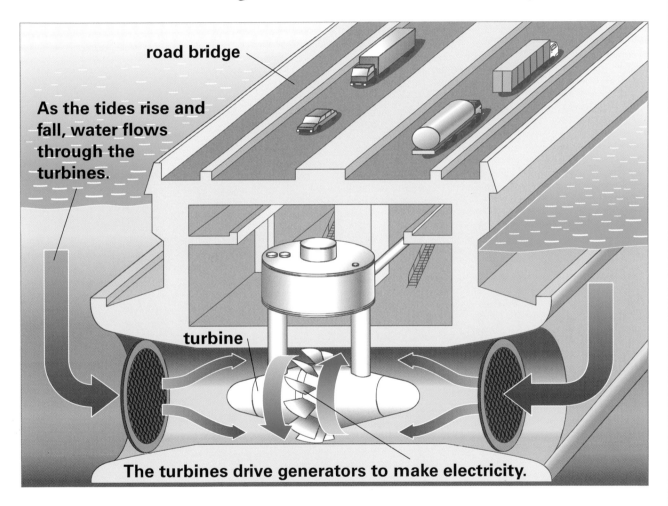

road bridge

As the tides rise and fall, water flows through the turbines.

turbine

The turbines drive generators to make electricity.

Although water power is a clean, non-**polluting** power source, it does create some problems. Valleys are often flooded to prepare for power plants. This means the loss of homes for both people and wildlife. Also, the tidal dams change the environment around rivers where many kinds of animals and birds live and breed.

SOLAR POWER

The Sun's energy is called solar energy. Solar means coming from the Sun. Solar energy can be changed into electricity inside special solar cells. These solar cells exist in many machines. Solar-powered calculators that you hold in your hand run on solar cells. Even buoys in the middle of the oceans and **satellites** in space depend on solar cells like these.

▼ *This large solar power plant is in New South Wales, Australia.*

It is possible to heat water for your home using a solar heater. This is a glass-covered box attached to the roof. Inside the box, pipes painted black absorb the Sun's heat and heat up the water flowing inside them.

PROJECT

Experience the power of solar heat!

You will need:
a few metres of hose
a tap
a bucket
a thermometer
a sunny day!

1. Lay the hose out in the sun.

2. Attach it to a tap and let it fill up with water.

3. Leave it for several hours in the sun.

4. Turn on the tap and run the water from the hose into a bucket. Take the temperature of the water in the bucket.

5. Run some more water directly from the tap and take its temperature. Compare the two temperatures. Which one is warmer?

Solar power is a very important energy source because we can always count on it. It does not **pollute** and it never ends.

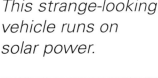

This strange-looking vehicle runs on solar power.

GEOTHERMAL POWER

It is also possible to draw out the heat energy from inside Earth. This is called **geothermal energy**. In many parts of the world, very hot rocks lie close to the surface. The temperature of these rocks can be as hot as 1000 °C. Sometimes this heat energy finds its way to the surface as hot springs or **geysers** that spout steam or water. We can use this hot water to produce electricity and heat buildings.

The Pohutu Geyser amazes visitors in New Zealand.

It is also possible to pump water down into Earth to be heated, and then return it to the surface to be used.

The Nesjavellir geothermal power plant in Iceland.

Geothermal power is a very clean energy source. Over twenty countries are now using it for at least some of their heat or electricity. Iceland is the largest user of geothermal energy in the world. About 85 per cent of all Iceland's homes are heated with geothermal water.

GLOSSARY

carnivore animal that lives on a diet of meat

chlorophyll green pigment found in plants

fossil fuels fuels formed over millions of years from the remains of living things. Coal, oil and natural gas are all fossil fuels.

generator device that changes movement energy into electricity

geothermal energy energy from the heat inside Earth

geyser natural fountain of hot water

hydroelectric power production of electricity using power obtained from the movement of water

kinetic energy energy an object has because it is moving

photosynthesis method by which plants make food using energy from the Sun

pollution substances that dirty or poison the land, sea and air

potential energy energy an object has because of the position it is in

satellite unmanned spacecraft in orbit around Earth

solar power power obtained from the energy of the Sun

turbine machine that is made to rotate to drive a generator